W9-ASB-967

DEC 1981

RECEIVED
OHIO DOMINICAN
COLLEGE LIBRARY
COLUMBUS, OHIO
43219

By Jane Sarnoff and Reynold Ruffins

S·P·A·C·E
A FACT AND RIDDLE BOOK

Text copyright © 1978 Jane Sarnoff   Illustrations copyright © 1978 Reynold Ruffins
Copyright under the Berne Convention. All rights reserved. No part of this book may be reproduced in any form without the permission of Charles Scribner's Sons.
Printed in the United States of America / Library of Congress Catalog Card Number 78-11499 / ISBN 0-684-15898-1
1 3 5 7 9 11 13 15 17 19 PD/C 20 18 16 14 12 10 8 6 4 2

Charles Scribner's Sons, New York

The Solar System

A solar system is made up of a sun and everything that revolves around it and travels with it through space. "Everything" can include planets and their satellites, asteroids, comets, meteors, dust, gases, and solar wind.

About 5 billion years ago our Sun and the nine planets that revolve around it were formed from a cloud of dust and gas. The huge cloud swirled into a tight mass, with a number of smaller masses and tiny particles breaking off. Most of the cloud became the Sun. As the largest body, the Sun provided the most gravitational pull and was able to keep the newly formed planets of our solar system in orbit around it. Some of the planets attracted smaller bodies—satellites or moons—that went into orbit around them.

All the planets revolve around the Sun in a counterclockwise direction and all orbit on almost the same plane. If you were to look at our solar system from far away, it would look flat. Other solar systems have planets in orbit in a number of different planes, so that from a distance they would look more like balls.

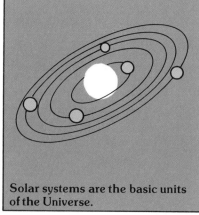

Solar systems are the basic units of the Universe.

In interplanetary space—the space between the planets—there are asteroids and comets in orbit around the Sun. Other comets travel to the outer limits of the solar system and swoop back to cut across planetary orbits. Meteoroids spin off from comets and asteroids, sometimes striking a moon or planet. Comets collide with each other, leaving dust and still more meteors.

Solar wind—tiny particles forced from the Sun's surface by heat—flows steadily throughout the solar system. Between and beyond the planets are small clouds of dust and cosmic debris, the remains of the material from which the solar system was made. And now, added to the natural debris, is the litter left by space exploration programs.

The Galaxy

A galaxy is a cluster of stars. Our solar system is part of a galaxy known as the Milky Way or just the Galaxy. It is a huge, flat, spiral wheel of more than 100 billion stars of different ages, sizes, and colors. What is often called the Milky Way is just our view of one edge of a spiral arm of our Galaxy. All of the approximately 5,000 stars that can be seen with the naked eye from Earth are part of the Milky Way galaxy. Between the stars there is gas and dust—some in clouds, some scattered. About 10 billion of the stars are thought to have planets in orbit around them.

Older galaxies, which no longer form new stars, are often oval in shape. Some galaxies are bar-shaped, others are formless masses of stars. A galaxy can contain from 1 billion to more than 1,000 billion stars. It has been estimated that there are about 10 billion galaxies in the Universe.

The center, or nucleus, of our spiral-shaped Galaxy is like a gigantic star. Around the nucleus is a tight ring of stars which thins out toward the arms of the spiral. The ring is made of the oldest stars in the Galaxy; the spiral arms of the Galaxy contain the youngest stars. Gases from intergalactic space—the area between galaxies—are drawn into the nucleus of the Milky Way and then stream away into the spiral arms. Once in the arms, the gases form the basis of new stars.

The entire Galaxy rotates at a speed of about 170 miles per second. The Galaxy is so big that a single rotation will take about 200 million years. Just as suns have planets and

J
520
S

planets have moons revolving around them, our Galaxy has two satellite galaxies revolving around it. The larger, the Magellanic Cloud, has about 20 billion stars; the Small Magellanic Cloud has about 2 billion stars. Scattered stars and gases connect the two cloud satellites with each other and with the Milky Way.

The Local Group

Our Milky Way Galaxy, another large spiral galaxy called the Great Galaxy of Andromeda, and about eighteen other galaxies make up a cluster of galaxies called the Local Group. All of the galaxies in the Local Group are moving together around a common center which is between the Andromeda Galaxy and the Milky Way. The entire galaxy cluster of the Local Group is equal in mass to about 500 billion stars and covers an area about 3 million light-years in diamater.

The part of space in which our galaxy cluster is located is rather empty. Deeper in space—at a distance more than twice the diameter of the Local Group—is an area called the Realm of Galaxies. Here there are clusters of many thousands of galaxies. Most of these galaxy clusters, along with our own Local Group, are part of a supergalaxy. The supergalaxy is a gigantic wheel of galaxy clusters rotating around a common center. There are other supergalaxies in space and there may even be clusters of supergalaxies formed into an even larger unit and rotating around a common center.

The Universe

According to most astronomers, space—the Universe or the cosmos—goes on and on forever. At one time, over 20 billion years ago, all the matter in the Universe was in one huge, tight ball. Then there was an explosion and all the materials from which the galaxies are made flew apart. Galaxies are still moving outward in all directions, away from each other, as a result of this explosion.

But what caused the explosion? And if the Universe is going on forever, growing ever larger, what is now in the space where the Universe will be? And will it ever end? There are no answers, only more theories. Perhaps we will find answers as astronauts explore more of space, as uncrewed spacecraft send back information from deeper in space. For now, however, the more we know about our own solar system, the more we can know about what might or might not be possible in other solar systems, other galaxies, supergalaxies, and beyond.

Our solar system (arrow) is at the edge of one arm of the Milky Way

115322

The Sun

The Milky Way is over 10 billion years old. The Sun, formed from a cloud of dust and gas within the Galaxy, is only 5 billion years old. As the cloud contracted—drew together—it got hotter and hotter and started to spin. As the pressure and temperature in the center increased, nuclear reactions began which made the gas ball even hotter. The new Sun quickly took on the characteristics it has today.

The Sun, like all stars, is made up of gases—mostly hydrogen and helium. At the center, or core, of the Sun, where energy is created, the gases are the thickest and the temperature the hottest: 15,000,000°K. (K stands for Kelvin, a method of measuring temperature that has −273° Centigrade as its lowest point. The temperature of the core of the Sun in Fahrenheit degrees is more than 27 million°.)

The next layer of the Sun, the convective zone, helps to move the energy outward. The continuous outward push of energy keeps the Sun from collapsing inward like a balloon when all the air rushes out. The gases in the second layer are thinner and not as hot as in the core of the Sun.

The third layer of the Sun, the photosphere, is the part of the Sun that we see from Earth. Here the gases are even thinner and the temperature is about 5,750°K. The photosphere is dotted with dark sunspots—large saucer-shaped areas where the temperature is only about 4,500°K. One astronaut who looked at the Sun through an indirect telescope while aboard a Skylab said it looked like a huge ball of oatmeal with pepper on it. (It is dangerous to look directly at the Sun—with or without a telescope.) There are storms on the Sun, often related to the sunspots, which affect activities on Earth.

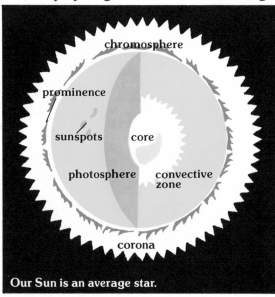

Our Sun is an average star.

Around the photosphere is a thin layer, visible only with a telescope, called the chromosphere. Enormous gas spurts—prominences—sometimes shoot hundreds of miles from the chromosphere into space. The chromosphere is surrounded by the corona, which is invisible, even through a telescope, except during an eclipse. The inner part of the corona is made of thin gases. The outer part is made of tiny particles that reflect the light of the Sun. Long solar streamers sometimes burst millions of miles into space from the corona. And it is from the corona that minute particles of gas are driven out into the solar system as solar wind. It takes energy more than 1 million years to travel from the Sun's core to its surface, but that energy, as light, reaches Earth in only 8 minutes and 20 seconds.

Most of the stars that can be seen from Earth with the unaided eye are brighter than the Sun. What makes the Sun seem so bright and large is its closeness. The Sun is 92,900,000 miles (149,475,000 kilometers) from Earth. There is 330,000 times as much material—mass—in the Sun as there is in the Earth. The diameter of the Sun is 864,000 miles (1,391,000 kilometers)—to form a ring around it, 350 Earths would be needed. The Sun takes almost a month to spin on its axis. Other stars, usually hotter ones, rotate in just a few hours.

When the Sun is compared to other stars it is only average in size, temperature, speed of rotation, and brightness. Because the Sun is average, and does not have rapid changes in motion or temperature, it has provided steady heat and light for a long enough time to allow life to evolve on Earth.

Why did the silly astronaut think he was so bright? Because his mother always called him sonny.

Why does the Sun always win arguments with the rain? Because it makes the rain dry up.

Which stars go to jail? Shooting stars.

What letter can move a star? The letter T can make a star start.

What has more nourishment, hamburger or a shooting star? A shooting star is meteor (meatier).

What is the best name for an astronomer? Stella.

How can you tune into a sun? Use a sundial.

What would the Sun be if I were in it and you were out of it? Sin.

Why are Lassie, Mickey Mouse, and a meteor the same? They are all stars with tails.

Whose business is often looking up in the worst of times? An astronomer's.

Why did the silly astronomer hit himself over the head in the morning? So he could see stars all day.

5

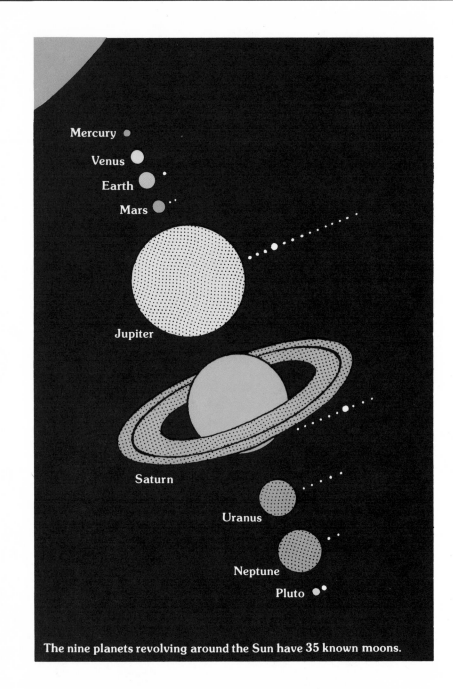

Mercury

Venus

Earth

Mars

Jupiter

Saturn

Uranus

Neptune

Pluto

The nine planets revolving around the Sun have 35 known moons.

The Planets

There are two groups of planets in the solar system—the inner planets and the outer or giant gas planets. The inner planets, also called terrestrial or earth-like, are Mercury, Venus, Earth, and Mars. These planets are rather small and solid or dense; they contain large amounts of iron and stone. The gas giants—Jupiter, Saturn, Uranus, and Neptune—are much larger and far less solid than the inner planets. They are swirling masses of gases that on an average are only as dense as water. The outer planets have many more satellites orbiting them than do the terrestrial planets.

Astronomers are not yet sure about the form of Pluto, the outermost planet. It is not a gas giant—it is even smaller than Mercury—and it is solid, but it is very lightweight in comparison to the inner planets. Pluto may not be the last planet in the solar system. Astronomers think there is likely to be another planet, perhaps two, orbiting the Sun beyond Pluto.

The planet nearest the Sun is Mercury; then comes Venus, Earth, Mars, Jupiter, Saturn, Uranus, Neptune, and Pluto. (To remember the order of the planets, learn this sentence: **M**y **V**ery **E**asy **M**ethod—**J**ust **S**et **U**p **N**ine **P**lanets.) Planets have no light of their own. They can be seen only because they reflect the Sun's light. Only Mercury, Venus, Mars, Jupiter, and Saturn reflect enough light to be seen, without a telescope, from Earth. Uranus, Neptune, and Pluto were discovered only after the invention of the telescope.

A planet's distance from the Sun affects the speed at which it revolves around the Sun. A planet close to the Sun revolves faster; one further out moves more slowly. Besides revolving around the Sun, each planet spins on its own axis—just as a top spins. Each completed spin is called a rotation. The trip around the Sun is the length of a planet's year. The time it takes a planet to rotate is the planet's day.

An astronaut had a brother who went to Pluto but the man who went to Pluto had no brother. How could this be? The astronaut was a woman.

What planet can we see most often without a telescope? The planet Earth.

What star looks brightest to an astronaut orbiting the Moon? The Sun.

Ruffins

Mercury

Mercury is the planet closest to the Sun. It is also a small planet for our solar system—just a bit bigger than our Moon. Mercury's size and closeness to the Sun mean that it is very hot and has too weak a gravitational pull to hold clouds and air—atmosphere—around it. There is no air on Mercury, no rain, no water at all. It can get as hot as 660°F (350°C) on the surface of the planet during the day and as cold as −270°F (−170°C) during the night.

Mercury turns completely on its axis every 58.65 earth-days and revolves around the Sun in 88 earth-days. Its average speed as it travels around, or orbits, the Sun is 30 miles per second. Once it was thought that Mercury always kept the same side toward the Sun, but radar observations and Mariner photographs showed that all of the surface of Mercury is turned toward the Sun at some time during its revolution.

The Mariner 10 space probe relayed much important new information about Mercury to Earth. The core of Mercury, like that of Earth, is probably made of iron or some other heavy material and is slightly magnetic. The surface of Mercury, however, is full of craters and smooth plains and looks more like the Moon than like the Earth.

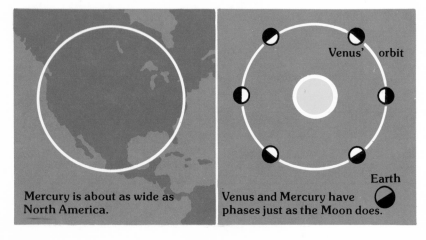

Mercury is about as wide as North America.

Venus and Mercury have phases just as the Moon does.

Venus

Venus is only slightly smaller than Earth and has about the same gravitational pull. Even though Venus is very close to Earth, it has been very difficult to find out much about its surface—Venus is always covered by clouds that float 60 miles above the surface. The clouds show that Venus does have an atmosphere, but Russian and United States space probes found that Venus' air is completely different from that of Earth. Earth's atmosphere is mostly nitrogen and oxygen and its clouds are water drops and ice crystals.

Venus has an atmosphere that is mostly carbon dioxide, with a small amount of water. Its clouds, also of carbon dioxide, are kept moving by winds of almost 200 miles per hour. The cloud cover reflects sunlight easily and makes Venus the third brightest body, after the Sun and the Moon, visible from Earth.

A Venusian year is 225 earth-days—the time it takes for the planet to travel around the Sun. But since it takes 243 earth-days for Venus to rotate on its axis, a Venusian day is longer than a Venusian year. Even more unusual is that Venus has been found, by radar studies, to rotate backwards. It spins on its axis in the opposite direction of all planets but Uranus, and opposite to the direction of its orbit.

Uncrewed Soviet space probes which landed on the planet sent back photographs that show a rocky surface. Other probes have found that the surface temperature is very high—about 1000°F (540°C). Radar images show that there is at least one lava flow about the size of the state of Nebraska.

Venus is a very smooth planet with few features more than a half a mile high or deep; however, astronomers believe that the probes and radar indicate that the type of mountain-building activity that shaped Earth, billions of years ago, is now going on on Venus.

How can you make your money go a long way? *By investing in space exploration.*

Which planet was the biggest before Jupiter was discovered? *Jupiter.*

Which ships are the hardest to conquer? *Hardships.*

What can you call a muddy spaceship that crosses the galaxy twice? *A dirty double-crosser.*

Why is foil to put over the top of a plate and the first person to find a planet the same? *They are both dish coverers.*

Why do you always find what you are looking for in the last place you look? *Because you stop looking when you find it.*

When did Venus begin with a V and end with an E? *Venus always began with a V and end always began with an E.*

Why did the space explorers call their last stop Fishhook? *Because it was at the end of the line.*

When has an astronaut going to Mars by spaceship the most reason to feel flat? *When he's a board.*

9

Earth

Earth is the third planet from the Sun. It takes Earth 365 days, 6 hours, 8 minutes, and 38 seconds to revolve around the Sun. Its average speed is 70,000 miles per hour. Each rotation of the Earth on its axis takes 23 hours, 56 minutes, and 4 seconds. Space-satellite measurements show that the Earth is *not* round. It is flattened slightly at each pole and has two indentations in the Northern Hemisphere.

The core of the Earth is solid iron and nickel, surrounded by liquid iron and nickel. The solid inner core has a diameter of 1,700 miles (2,750 kilometers); the liquid outer core is about 1,300 miles thick (2,100 kilometers). The cores create an unseen magnetic field that extends thousands of miles into space. Surrounding the core is an area called the mantle, which is about 1,800 miles thick (2,900 kilometers) and is made of rock. Then comes the continental crust, with an average thickness of 23 miles (37 kilometers). Finally, the surface of Earth: the oceanic crust with an average thickness of 4 miles (6.5 kilometers). Earth can be considered a water-covered planet since water covers 70 percent of the surface and goes to an average depth of 12,700 feet (3,870 meters). The average height of the land above sea level is only 2,700 feet (825 meters).

All around the globe that is the planet Earth and reaching out for a hundred miles are the gases that make up its atmosphere—nitrogen, oxygen, argon, carbon dioxide, and great amounts of water vapor that condenses into clouds. This atmosphere was not there when the planet first formed and cooled. Volcanic activity may have produced the nitrogen, carbon dioxide, and water vapor; decay and natural radioactivity could have provided some of the other atmospheric elements. Plants, which need carbon dioxide to live, let off the oxygen which animals need to live. It is likely that before plants developed there was no oxygen in our atmosphere. Carbon dioxide helped to trap the heat of the Sun during the night so that temperatures did not change too greatly for developing life forms. (The average temperature of the Earth is 70°F (21°C).)

The oceanic crust and part of the lower atmosphere form an area called the biosphere—where life can exist. Life forms on Earth are now plentiful and varied. They range from single-celled plants and animals to complex organisms of both types. There is life in the oceans and on the land. Some Earth organisms have even left their planet to explore its outer space and visit its only natural satellite, the Moon.

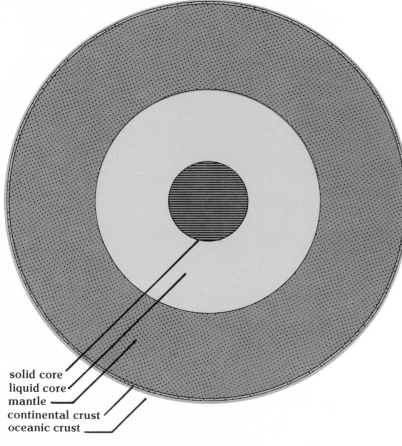

solid core
liquid core
mantle
continental crust
oceanic crust

Earth weighs approximately 6,588,000,000,000,000,000,000 tons.

Why don't sophisticated people go to the Moon for vacations? Because it doesn't have the right atmosphere.

Why did the moon-to-planet shuttle captain change jobs? Her work made her cross all the time.

What came into being at the same time as the Earth, will probably exist as long as the Earth, but is never more than 5 weeks old? The Moon.

When was beef the highest ever?
When the cow jumped over the Moon.

What part of the Moon is in the Sun?
The letter N.

When is it impossible to land on the Moon?
When it is full.

What heavenly body has lots of dimes and nickels?
The Moon, it is always changing quarters.

What did the Swiss cheese say to the man-in-the-Moon?
I'm holier than thou.

Why didn't the astronaut hurt himself when he fell out of the lunar module?
He wasn't hurt until he landed on the Moon.

Earth's Satellite: The Moon

The Moon is an average distance of 239,000 miles (384,000 kilometers) from Earth. Its orbit around the Earth is not circular, but elliptical or oval-shaped. When the Moon is closest to Earth, it is 221,463 miles away. That point on the orbit is called the perigee. When the Moon is at its greatest distance from Earth—the apogee of the orbit—it is 252,710 miles away. (All distances are measured from the center of the Earth to the center of the Moon.) It takes the Moon 27 days, 7 hours, and 43.2 minutes to travel around the Earth. The Moon does not, however, travel around the Earth at a uniform rate. It goes fastest when it is closest to Earth and slowest when it is farthest away.

While the Moon is revolving around Earth, it is rotating on its axis. Because it turns on its axis at almost the same rate at which it travels around the Earth, the same half of the Moon is always facing Earth. The position of the Moon in relation to the Sun and the Earth is what makes it appear full or new from Earth.

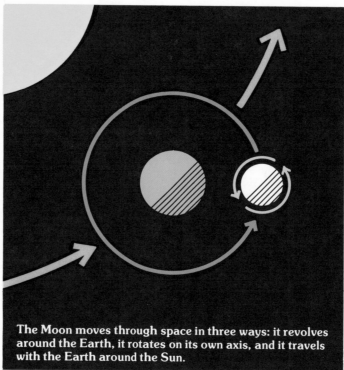

The Moon moves through space in three ways: it revolves around the Earth, it rotates on its own axis, and it travels with the Earth around the Sun.

Like the Earth and the other planets, the Moon has no light of its own and can be seen only because it reflects the light of the Sun. When the Moon is between the Earth and the Sun, only a thin crescent of the Moon can reflect the light of the Sun and be seen on Earth. As it moves around the Earth, the Sun's light falls on more and more of the side of the Moon facing Earth. The Moon is seen as full when the Earth is between the Sun and the Moon and the entire side of the Moon facing Earth can reflect the light of the Sun.

The full moon is not twice as bright as the half moon. Instead it is almost nine times as bright. This is because a smooth surface reflects more light than a rough surface and the part of the Moon that can be seen as a half moon is very rough and mountainous. The part of the Moon that makes up the other half of the full moon is mostly flat plains, which reflect light very well. Where the Sun shines on the Moon, temperatures can rise to over 500°F (260°C). In areas where the Sun is not shining on the Moon, the temperatures can go as low as −220°F (−140°C).

The surface of the moon is a combination of deep depressions — craters or pits — long mountain ranges with tall peaks, and wide plains. Some of the mountains are taller than the tallest on Earth. The first photographs of the far side of the Moon, taken from the U.S.S.R. spacecraft Lunik III, showed that that side has more mountains and fewer plains than the near side of the Moon.

The Moon is about 1/4 the size of Earth and it has no atmosphere. Its mass is only about 1/80th that of Earth and its gravitational pull is only 1/6 that of Earth. Astronauts who landed on the Moon weighed only 1/6 the amount they did on Earth. Someone who weighed 162 pounds on Earth would only weigh 27 pounds on the Moon; someone who weighed 60 pounds on Earth would only weigh 10 pounds.

The Apollo astronauts brought back samples of Moon rocks that contained many known Earth minerals and three new minerals. Some elements that are scarce on Earth were found to be plentiful on the Moon; other common elements on Earth were found to be almost absent from lunar rocks. Most of the rocks brought back by the astronauts were formed about 3.5 billion years ago. But one rock brought back from the Apollo 12 mission is 4.6 billion years old — the oldest rock ever found on the Moon or the Earth.

When astronauts Armstrong and Aldrin walked on the Moon they kept slipping on the Moon dust. The dust they brought back was looked at under a microscope that enlarged it 7,000 times. Almost every piece was a tiny ball. Walking on the Moon is like walking on millions of miniature ball bearings.

Geologists have one theory to explain the reason for the round dust: it is possible that over the course of the Moon's development, when it was still not solid, meteorites smashed into it. Great amounts of melted materials from the Moon were splashed miles above the surface. Like all fluids in free fall, the melted material took a round shape and then hardened and became solid as it fell back to the surface. There the round dust lay for billions of years…until the arrival of astronauts Armstrong and Aldrin on July 20, 1969, at 4:17 P.M., EDT. They were the first people to walk on the Moon. And, because there is no rain to wash them away and no wind to fill them with dust, their footprints — slipmarks and all — will remain for thousands of years.

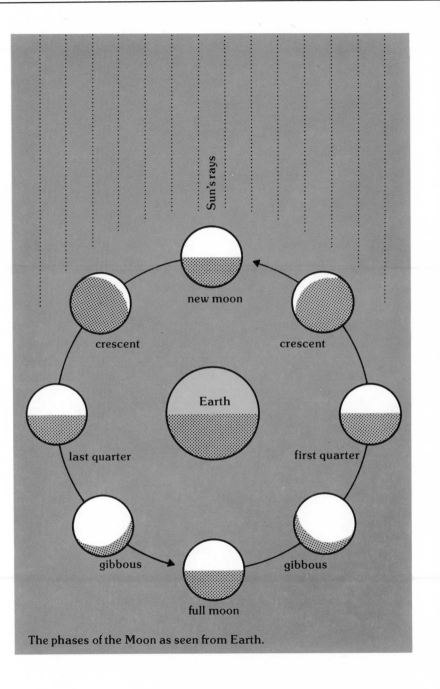

The phases of the Moon as seen from Earth.

What did the space cook see on the skillet?
Unidentified frying objects.

What dish is out of this world?
A flying saucer.

What is an astronaut?
Someone who is glad to be down and out.

Why was the tree petrified when the spaceship landed?
The impact made it rock.

Why is the sky cleaner on planets with a lot of tall cities?
Because there are more skyscrapers.

How do you know that people are smarter in the country than in the city?
Because the population is always denser in the city.

What do you call a hot-rod space shuttle that won't run?
A shot rod.

What can you eat that nobody on Earth ever saw before?
Break open a peanut shell and eat the nut.

Why is a parachute like an apple?
They both have to do with the fall of man.

Who always falls down on the job?
A parachuter.

Why won't the world ever come to an end?
Because it is round.

Mars

Mars is about twice the size of the Moon and half that of the Earth. Its diameter at the equator is 4,217 miles (6,785 kilometers). Mars takes 687 days to revolve around the Sun, at an average distance of 141,500,000 miles (226,673,500 kilometers) and an average speed of 15 miles per second. Mars rotates on its axis in 24 hours, 39 minutes, and 35 seconds. A Martian day is, therefore, just a little longer than an earth-day but its year is more than twice as long as an earth-year.

Mars has a layer of thin, whitish clouds that show the presence of an atmosphere. But the Martian atmosphere is only about one percent as thick as Earth's and is mostly carbon dioxide. The average temperature on Mars is −45°F (−43°C). The hottest it ever gets is about 77°F (25°C) — at noon at the equator. The worst part of the weather on Mars is the wind. Fierce winds create hurricane-like storms that blow dust at 300 m.p.h.

The surface of the planet is mostly red in color, with rather large dark areas that early astronomers mistakenly thought were seas. Like Earth, Mars has polar ice caps which grow smaller when near the Sun. The Viking orbiters found that the caps are made of frozen water, not frozen carbon dioxide as had been believed. Russian and United States uncrewed probe missions to Mars provided much information about the surface of the planet. Almost half the surface is heavily cratered. The other half has huge, inactive volcanos, vast canyons, gullies, and narrow channels. Although Mars now has a dry surface, there is evidence of ancient river beds and of the presence of large amounts of water deep inside the planet. One of the volcanic mountains, Mt. Olympica, is the largest known mountain in the solar system. It is over 300 miles (483 kilometers) in diameter and over 15 miles (24 kilometers) high.

Mars' moons may be asteroids captured by the planet's gravitational force.

Mars has two moons, Phobos and Deimos. Phobos, the largest and nearest, is oval, 17 miles (27 kilometers) long, and revolves around Mars twice in each Martian-day from a distance of 3,700 miles (5,955 kilometers) above the surface. Phobos is the only moon of any planet that revolves around its planet in a shorter time than the planet's day. Phobos is also unlike other moons in that it is slowly moving toward the surface of the planet and radar studies show that it has some of the traits of a hollow body. Some scientists have considered the possibility that Phobos is an artificial moon. Deimos is only 10 miles (16 kilometers) long. It revolves around Mars in 30 hours, 18 minutes from a distance of 12,500 miles (20,115 kilometers) above the surface. Both moons are deeply pitted by meteorites from the many asteroids orbiting the Sun in this space between Mars and Jupiter.

Viking 1 and 2 landed on Mars on July 20 and September 3, 1976, respectively. They were the first spacecraft ever sent to another planet to find out if there is life on it. Even with all the information they and other Mars space missions have gathered, scientists are still not sure if there is life on Mars. If there is life on Mars, however, it is very different from any life form on Earth.

Jupiter

Jupiter is big. If it were hollow all the other planets in the solar system would fit inside it. But Jupiter is not hollow — it contains more matter than all the other planets, moons, asteroids, gas, dust, and debris in the solar system combined. Its diameter at the equator is 89,000 miles (143,200 kilometers), about eleven times that of Earth. Although Jupiter is the largest of the planets, it has the shortest day: it rotates on its axis in only 9 hours and 51 minutes. Jupiter takes almost 12 earth-years, however, to complete its orbit around the Sun, moving at 8.1 miles per second, which is slow compared to the inner planets.

Jupiter, the first of the gas giants, is very different from the four inner planets. Its atmosphere, which is mostly hydrogen with some helium, methane, and ammonia, is too thick to allow observation of the surface. But there may be no solid surface to Jupiter. It is possible that the entire planet is a thick, hot, liquid hydrogen with only a very small solid core. There is probably no sharp division between the hydrogen atmosphere and the hydrogen ocean. At the "surface" level, temperatures of 800°F (427°C) have been recorded by the uncrewed Pioneer space probe. Temperatures below surface level reach 12,000°F (6,650°C) — hotter than the surface of the Sun. The measurements were taken by the space probes from the planet's outer atmosphere: spacecraft must stay far away from the surface of Jupiter or be destroyed by the heat.

Telescopes show an oval red spot — the Great Red Spot — moving in a counterclockwise direction in the atmosphere above the cloud cover. It is a whirling column 17,000 miles (27,350 kilometers) long and 8,000 miles (12,875 kilometers) wide. Scientists think it is a storm, at least 300 years old, that will disappear in time. Most of the planet is stormy, with high winds and lightning among clouds fifty miles high.

Around the equator are bands of light and dark gas. Different types of radio signals have been recorded from Jupiter which were at first related to the Red Spot and the gas bands and were thought to be mysterious. They have been found to be caused by the natural movement of electrons throughout the planet's atmosphere.

Jupiter has fourteen satellites, four of which are large moons. The largest of the moons, Ganymede, is bigger than the planet Mercury. The other three moons are the size of Earth's moon and one, Io, has an atmosphere of its own. While astronauts may never be able to land on Jupiter, they may be able to land on one of its moons. The other ten satellites are very small — some less than ten miles across. Four of them may be asteroids from the space between Mars and Jupiter that were captured by Jupiter's strong gravitational pull.

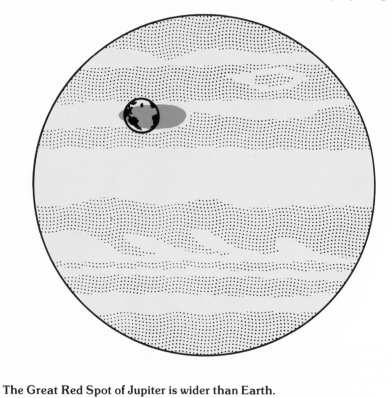

The Great Red Spot of Jupiter is wider than Earth.

What stays down when it flies up?

A feather.

What is as big as a spaceship but weighs nothing?

The spaceship's shadow.

When do we weigh the least?

During the day, when the sun is shining, everything is a bit lighter.

How can you prove that heat makes things expand and cold contracts them?

On every planet summer days are long and winter days are short.

What has no sides and no thickness but can still be measured?

The temperature.

What weighs very little but cannot be lifted by the strongest creature?

A bubble.

What exercise is best to help you lose weight?

Pushing yourself away from the table.

What always weighs the same whether it is made larger or smaller?

A hole.

What liquid will never freeze?

Boiling water.

Saturn

Saturn is the second largest planet in the solar system, but it is a very lightweight planet. Like Jupiter, Saturn is mostly gases with a very small solid core. The gases that make up Saturn, however, are of a lighter weight than those of Jupiter. Even its atmosphere is of the lightest gases. If there were a body of water big enough, Saturn would be able to float in it.

Saturn is 886 million miles (1,385 million kilometers) from the Sun. It takes 29½ earth-years to travel around the Sun, but only 10 hours and 14 minutes to rotate on its axis.

Revolving around Saturn's equator is a system of rings made of ice or ice-covered rocks. The rocks are probably small pieces of a satellite of Saturn that broke apart millions of years ago. The rings go out from the planet about 85,000 miles (136,400 kilometers), but they are only about 10 miles (16 kilometers) thick. The rings do not revolve around Saturn as a solid band; each of the many billions of particles of ice and rock moves at its own speed. The particles closer to the planet move faster than the particles that form the outer edges of the rings. The ring system is divided into four separate rings by the gravitational forces of Saturn's ten, or possibly eleven, moons. One of the moons, Titan, is one of the largest satellites in the solar system—just a bit smaller than Mars. It has its own atmosphere and a surface pressure similar to that of Earth. Another of Saturn's moons, Phoebe, is one of the six satellites in the solar system that revolves in the opposite direction that its planet revolves.

Uranus

Before 1781, the Sun was thought to have only six planets. Then stronger telescopes were developed and Uranus was discovered to be orbiting beyond Saturn.

Like Saturn, Uranus is a giant planet made mostly of hydrogen and having rings and moons. The planet rotates in 10 hours and 50 minutes, and so its day is about the same length as a day on Jupiter or Saturn. Uranus is about 32,000 miles (51,500 kilometers) in diameter. It rotates in the opposite direction from all the other planets, except Venus. During its orbit, which takes 84 earth-years to complete, Uranus moves

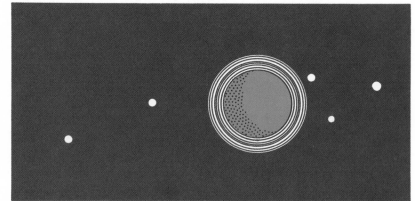

Saturn and Uranus (here seen from above) are both orbited by multiple rings.

1,783 million miles (2,870 million kilometers) from the Sun. As might be expected, temperatures are very low, with an average of −310°F (−155°C). Much of the information we have about Uranus has been collected by balloon satellite measurements made high in the Earth's atmosphere.

Uranus has eight rings of ice or iron, most of which move in a regular orbit around the planet. One ring, however, is narrow at some points, wide at others, and moves around the planet like a lopsided hula hoop. Uranus has five moons, which may be ice-covered, that revolve around the planet outside the rings. The largest of the moons, Titania, is about 700 miles (1,125 kilometers) in diameter.

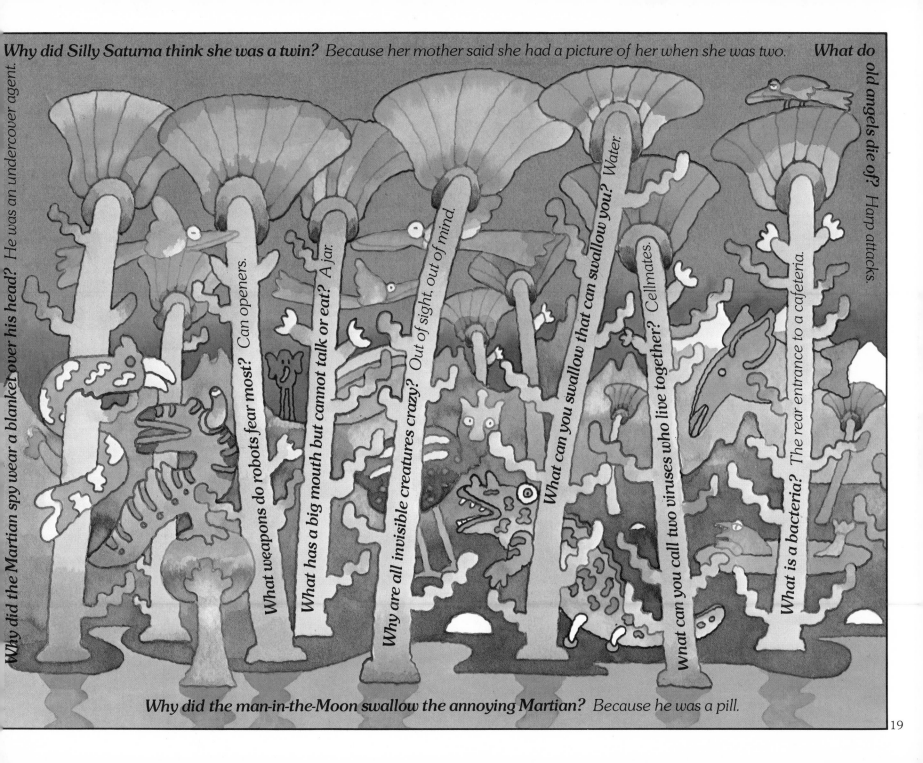

Why did Silly Saturna think she was a twin? Because her mother said she had a picture of her when she was two.

What do old angels die of? Harp attacks.

Why did the Martian spy wear a blanket over his head? He was an undercover agent.

What weapons do robots fear most? Can openers.

What has a big mouth but cannot talk or eat? A jar.

Why are all invisible creatures crazy? Out of sight, out of mind.

What can you swallow that can swallow you? Water.

What can you call two viruses who live together? Cellmates.

What is a bacteria? The rear entrance to a cafeteria.

Why did the man-in-the-Moon swallow the annoying Martian? Because he was a pill.

19

Neptune

After Uranus was discovered, astronomers followed its movements for many years and saw that its path was not one that could be expected according to the newly determined laws of gravity. They reasoned that the gravity of a planet even further out in space might be pulling Uranus away from the Sun. The astronomers calculated where such a planet might be located and, in 1846, looked in that area of the sky with the best telescope then available. Neptune was just where they expected the planet to be.

Neptune is the fourth of the gas giants. It is very much like Uranus in form and atmosphere. Of course, little is known about Neptune since it is so far away and since, like the other gas giants, it has a cloud cover. It is known that Neptune is very close in size to Uranus but that it is slightly denser. Neptune is much further out from the Sun than Uranus: its orbit takes it 2,790 million miles (4,490 million kilometers) from the Sun and takes 165 earth-years to complete. Neptune's day is 15 hours and 50 minutes.

Neptune has two known moons. The larger, Triton, is almost the size of Jupiter's Ganymede and Saturn's Titan. Neptune's other moon is very small in comparison—less than 200 miles (320 kilometers) in diameter. Triton travels around the planet every 5.8 earth-days, but the smaller moon takes 360 earth-days to complete the trip. There may be other moons in orbit around Neptune that are too small to detect, even with modern equipment.

Pluto

Pluto was not discovered until 1930. Powerful telescopes and photographic equipment were necessary to locate it since it is small—smaller than Mercury—and very far out in the solar system. It is about 40 times as far from the Sun as the Earth is. From the surface of Pluto the Sun would look like a large, bright star. Pluto revolves around the Sun once every 248 earth-years. Its orbit is long and narrow and not as regular as are the orbits of most of the planets. During part of its trip it even moves closer to the Sun than Neptune does.

Some astronomers think that Pluto might be a runaway moon of Neptune or a large chip off the planet. Pluto has been found to be very light in weight, even for such a small planet: it weighs about 1/8 as much as Earth's moon.

In 1978 a satellite was sighted orbiting Pluto. The moon is very close to the surface of the planet—20 times as close as Earth's moon to its surface. The moon, which has been named Charon, is over 1/3 the diameter of Pluto, and it has only about 1/10 the weight of the planet. It takes Charon almost the same time to revolve around Pluto that it takes the planet to rotate — about 6 earth-days. Someone on Pluto would, therefore, always see the moon in the same place in the sky; someone on the far side of the planet would never see the moon at all. Because of the moon's size and closeness to Pluto, the two bodies look like two planets revolving together around the Sun.

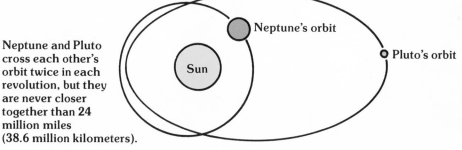

Neptune and Pluto cross each other's orbit twice in each revolution, but they are never closer together than 24 million miles (38.6 million kilometers).

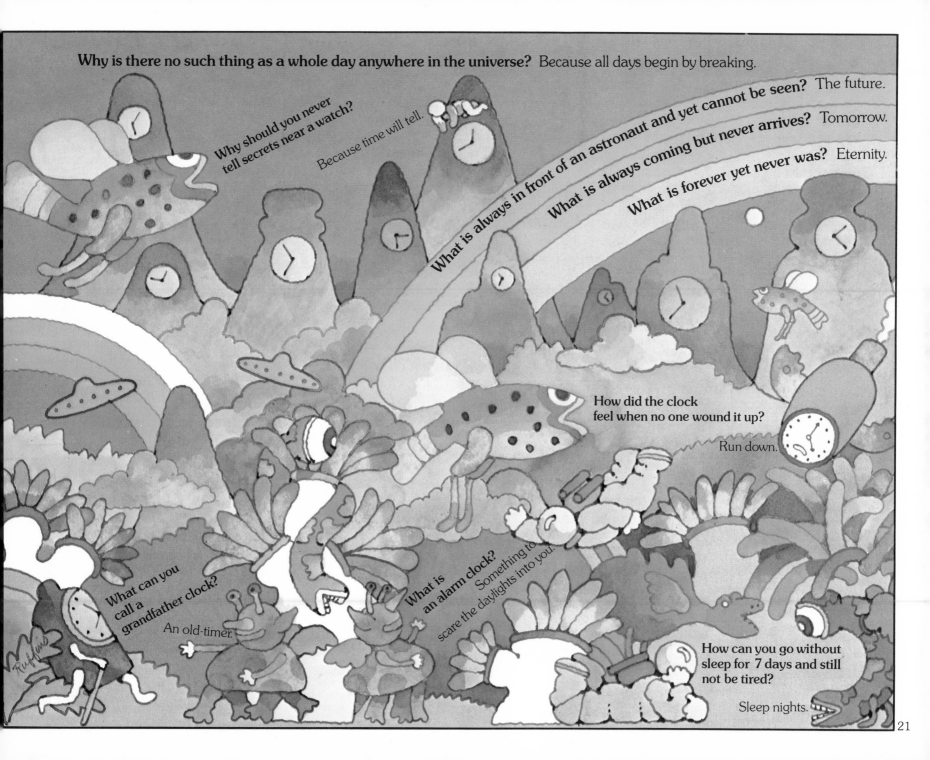

Why is there no such thing as a whole day anywhere in the universe? Because all days begin by breaking.

Why should you never tell secrets near a watch? Because time will tell.

What is always in front of an astronaut and yet cannot be seen? The future.

What is always coming but never arrives? Tomorrow.

What is forever yet never was? Eternity.

How did the clock feel when no one wound it up? Run down.

What can you call a grandfather clock? An old-timer.

What is an alarm clock? Something to scare the daylights into you.

How can you go without sleep for 7 days and still not be tired? Sleep nights.

Asteroids: The Minor Planets

Between Mars and Jupiter is a gap of 350 million miles (565 million kilometers). There is more than enough room in the gap for one or two more planets. Early astronomers expected to find a planet in orbit between the fourth and fifth planets, but when the newly discovered telescopes were trained on the gap, the space appeared empty. Then, on the first night of the nineteenth century, a very small planet was sighted. The planet was Ceres, less than 500 miles (800 kilometers) in diameter, yet still the largest of the asteroids or minor planets that orbit in space between Mars and Jupiter.

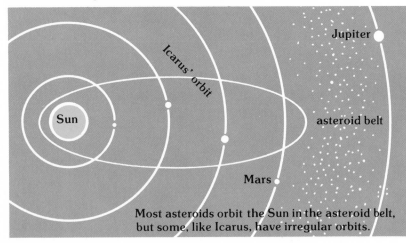

Most asteroids orbit the Sun in the asteroid belt, but some, like Icarus, have irregular orbits.

There are nearly 30,000 other asteroids that are considered "large." They range from 300 miles (480 kilometers) in diameter to about the size of a medium-sized mountain. Icarus, one of the best-known asteroids, is about one mile (1.6 kilometers) in diameter. In addition, there are millions of asteroids the size of huge rocks, small stones, and even grains of sand.

At first it was thought that the asteroids were the remains of a planet that had exploded, or of two planets that had collided. But that is unlikely since if all the asteroids were put together they would form a planet less than 1/1000 the size of Earth. It is now thought that the asteroids are made of the original dust from which the Sun and its planets were made. The material formed into small bodies but did not become attached to any of the larger spheres.

Sixteen hundred of the larger asteroids have been followed telescopically by astronomers to plot their orbits. All of them move around the Sun in the same west-to-east direction as the other planets. Most, but not all, of the asteroids stay in orbit between Mars and Jupiter. Jupiter controls, by gravitational pull, a group of asteroids called the Trojans. Some of them follow Jupiter's orbit, staying about one-sixth of an orbit behind the planet. Another Trojan group is in Jupiter's orbit but moving in front of the planet. Jupiter has a very strong gravitational pull, especially in comparison with the much smaller Mars. Sometimes Jupiter pulls an asteroid out of the asteroid belt and sends it off on a new orbit. Some move sunward, others toward space. Which ever direction their orbits take, however, sooner or later they again cross orbits with Jupiter and get captured by its pull. They are then either returned to orbit within the asteroid belt or are once more sent out in a new orbit.

Some asteroids do not orbit in the asteroid belt between Mars and Jupiter but have very irregular orbits. Icarus, for example, is now in an orbit that takes it from the asteroid belt to far inside Mercury's orbit. Another asteroid, Hermes, is in an orbit which might allow it to pass between the Moon and the Earth. Asteroids that cross Earth's orbit are called Apollo asteroids. There are nineteen known Apollo asteroids.

Craters and star wounds — astroblems — on the planets and their satellites show where asteroids have crashed. Many boulder-sized asteroids collide with Earth each year, but they do little damage. Larger asteroids, the size of mountains, are thought to collide with Earth at most once every 10,000 years.

Can you spell eighty in two letters?

A.T.

What is both the beginning of eternity and the end of time and space?

The letter E.

The English alphabet goes from A to Z. What goes from Z to A?

A zebra.

Can you use "I is" correctly in a sentence?

I is the letter that comes after H.

How can you get rid of varnish?

Take away its R.

What single word means both dumb and smart?

Wisdom.

Can you spell very smart in two letters?

YY spells 2 ys.

What vowel makes the most noise?

O. The rest are in-audible.

What word is nothing, but when you take away one letter you still have one?

None.

What can speak every language on every world but has never been to school?

An echo.

Rukkins

23

Comets

Deep in space, far beyond the orbit of Pluto but still centered on the Sun, there may be a cloud of comets. The comets are small—from less than a mile to several miles in diameter—and are probably made of frozen gases, small rock fragments, and dust. From time to time comets leave the comet cloud and move toward the center of the solar system. They follow a long, thin, oval orbit with one end of the oval often far in space and the other crossing the planets' orbits.

The comets we are most familiar with are periodic comets—comets that are kept by gravitational forces in a relatively short oval or elliptical orbit around the Sun. Comets that are not trapped into such a short orbit around the Sun sometimes make a single appearance and then disappear into deep space. The most well-known of the periodic comets is Halley's Comet. It nears the Sun and can be seen from Earth every 76.1 years. Halley's Comet was first seen, or its presence was first recorded, by Japanese and Chinese astronomers in 240 B.C. May 1986 is its closest date of appearance.

As a comet nears the Sun its frozen gases turn into vapor—almost a fog that is neither liquid nor solid. A bubble of dust and gas, called a coma or head, is formed around the icy core. The head of the comet may be 500,000 miles (804,500 kilometers) wide. If the comet is in an orbit which brings it close enough to the Sun, the heat may cause a double tail to trail out more than 10 million miles (16 million kilometers) in space.

One part of the tail is gas; the other part, shorter and wider, is made of dust. Sunlight shines in the scattered dust and is reflected by the gas, making the comet easily seen by telescope if not by the naked eye. Recently it has been found that comets are surrounded by an enormous cloud of hydrogen that may be ten times the size of the Sun.

Comets that travel too close to the Sun have been known to split apart and rain meteors onto nearby planets. A comet which appeared regularly every 6½ years split in 1846. It appeared in 1852 as two comets moving in orbit side by side and then disappeared. Twenty years later meteors from the double comet appeared in Earth's atmosphere. The burning meteors were seen all over Europe as a blazing star shower.

In 1908 a comet that was not broken up by the sun or destroyed by the friction of entering the atmosphere collided with Earth in Siberia. Trees thirty miles from the site of impact

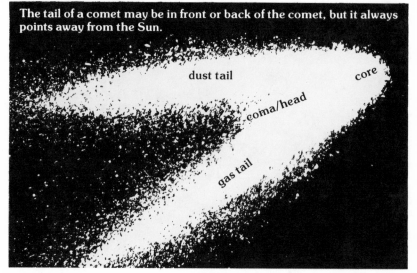

The tail of a comet may be in front or back of the comet, but it always points away from the Sun.

dust tail

coma/head

core

gas tail

were uprooted, land shook 400 miles (645 kilometers) from the site. The pressure of the blast was recorded as far away as England. Smoke from the explosion traveled to the upper atmosphere and made sunsets particularly long and colorful for many weeks. The comet was small compared to other wanderers—only about a mile in diameter and a million tons in weight. The explosion on impact was so great because of the unusual speed at which the comet struck the planet—25 miles per second.

Meteors

Meteors are small bits of matter that enter Earth's atmosphere at high speeds. They become visible from Earth when they are about 75 miles (120 kilometers) above the surface of the planet. They burn as they pass through the atmosphere and look, as they are often called, like falling or shooting stars.

Some meteors—called sporadic meteors—are the result of a comet exploding or falling apart. Small pieces of the comet are sent in all directions—some to the outer limits of the solar system, some toward the Sun. If a piece of the comet passes near enough to a planet it can be attracted by gravitational forces and pulled into the planet's atmosphere. Sporadic meteors are common and can be seen on any clear night as they enter the Earth's atmosphere. Some sporadic meteors may be parts of asteroids rather than comets.

Periodic meteors are the dust left by a comet's wake. As the Earth turns, it attracts the dust that a comet leaves behind. The dust is pulled into the atmosphere and, as the many hundreds of pieces burn, they look like a shower of falling stars.

Astronomers know when meteor showers are going to occur since each shower is related to the passing of a particular comet. In May there is a meteor shower called the Aquarids, which may be associated with Halley's Comet. The Perseids appear each August and are associated with a comet that passed Earth in 1862. Each year as Earth passes the place on its orbit nearest the comet's wake, dust is collected, pulled into the atmosphere, and burned out, providing a spectacular show for the sky watchers.

Meteors usually burn or are turned into vapor by heat and friction as they enter Earth's atmosphere. Only the harmless remains of most meteors drift to the surface of the planet. The pieces of larger meteors that do not burn in the atmosphere but fall to Earth are called meteorites. About 500 meteorites fall on Earth each year. Meteorites that weigh 70 tons have struck Earth. Meteorites, the remains of meteors, asteroids, and other space debris fall to Earth and add almost two million tons of material to the planet each year. Most of this material cannot be distinguished from terrestrial material.

Some scientists have suggested that life on Earth began when a comet or meteorite struck Earth. Molecules and chemicals necessary to the start of life have been found on some meteorites and on at least one comet. And some medical scientists believe that it is possible that extraterrestrial—non-earth—life forms "invade" Earth as the planet passes through the dust of comets and as meteoric debris falls through the atmosphere. Influenza and even the common cold, which does not seem to have existed on Earth before the fifteenth century, may have been carried to Earth by a meteorite.

The many craters on the Moon show how often the Moon has been struck by meteorites. Some astronomers believe that the Moon was hit by a gigantic meteorite 800 years ago and that it is still wobbling from the impact. In June 1178, English monks reported that a "flaming torch" suddenly leapt from the crescent moon, sending out "…fire, hot coals, and sparks." Astronomers think that the monks saw a meteorite hit the Moon and that one of the newest craters on the Moon is the site of the impact. Information relayed by Soviet and United States equipment at lunar landing sites seem to show an irregularity in the moon's rotation. The Moon has a wobble of twenty-five to thirty feet (9 to 10½ meters) that may be due to the meteorite.

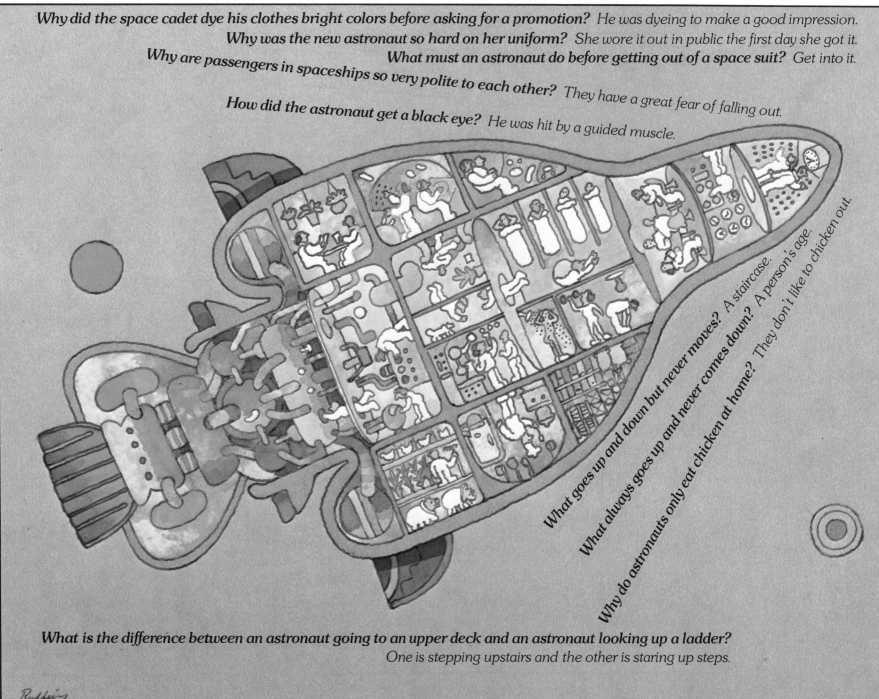

Why did the space cadet dye his clothes bright colors before asking for a promotion? *He was dyeing to make a good impression.*

Why was the new astronaut so hard on her uniform? *She wore it out in public the first day she got it.*

What must an astronaut do before getting out of a space suit? *Get into it.*

Why are passengers in spaceships so very polite to each other? *They have a great fear of falling out.*

How did the astronaut get a black eye? *He was hit by a guided muscle.*

What goes up and down but never moves? *A staircase.*

What always goes up and never comes down? *A person's age.*

Why do astronauts only eat chicken at home? *They don't like to chicken out.*

What is the difference between an astronaut going to an upper deck and an astronaut looking up a ladder?
One is stepping upstairs and the other is staring up steps.

Living in Space

The astronauts and scientists who crewed the United States Skylab and the Russian Salyut space stations stayed in space for weeks, even months. The problems they faced and the ways in which those problems were solved make it clear that it is possible to live in space. It is likely that in the near future, perhaps even before the end of the century, there will be a permanent space station revolving around Earth.

Scientists and astronauts are the explorers and investigators of space. The next group of people to go into space will probably be construction and maintenance workers: they will be building a solar power station. The station will have to be built in space because nothing so large could be launched directly from Earth. Once built, the station will trap energy from the Sun and beam it toward Earth for use as electricity. About 1,500 workers would be needed to complete the first stage of the station. But that many people would need others to take care of them—doctors, nurses, dentists, engineers, even cooks and cleaners. And if workers stayed for long periods—increasing the size and uses of the station—they would want their families with them. That would mean more housing — and so more construction workers — more medical staff, hospitals, schools, teachers, shops, and recreation areas. The population of the station would probably grow quickly to be about 3,000 to 5,000—a small town in space.

Soon after the solar station is built, people will realize how simple living in space can be. A larger station—a space colony—will then be built. The colony might have a population of many tens of thousands of people. It would be a small city rather than a small town. The best place for such a colony, scientists think, would be in orbit midway between the Earth and the Moon. There the colony would not be exposed to the dangers of deeper space and could be easily linked to Earth

— the Old World — by space shuttles. Some scientists think that the colony will be a huge hollow ball with the colonists living inside. Other scientists see the future colony as a giant wheel with colonists living inside the rim. Materials from the Moon and the asteroids might be used in the construction of the colony.

The design for any space colony will have to include the creation of an artifical gravity. Because the human body was developed for and by the effects of gravity, weightlessness can cause many physical and practical problems. The astronauts found just how difficult it is for humans to live completely without gravity and yet how helpful lowered gravity could be for some activities. In either the ball or wheel station, the living quarters would be in earth-gravity areas. So would schools, shops, farms, offices, "traditional" recreation areas, and some factories and laboratories. Other factories, where heavy equipment is necessary, laboratory facilities, and "new style" recreation areas would be in parts of the station with lower gravity, where people and things would weigh less.

Both types of station would be so big that you could not see from one side to the other. Polished metal plates would reflect light inside the stations and control the amount of heat.

Weather would be "manufactured" and there would be rain only at night. Seeds, trees, animals, birds, and fish would all be shipped from Earth. Pests — mosquitos, poison ivy, and disease-causing bacteria—could all be kept off the station. Of course, solar energy would be used to produce electric power.

Weightlessness or reduced gravity would make the station very different from Earth. Blood flow, muscle use, vision—all our body systems—can change during even short periods of weightlessness. Special training and exercise will be necessary for people who spend much time in reduced-gravity areas. Children born on the colony will probably have less trouble going back and forth between areas with different levels of gravity. After a few generations the standard gravity of the station might be reduced to less than earth-gravity to suit those born in space.

Sports in the weightless area would be very different from sports at earth-gravity. New games would have to be developed, especially new ball games. To overcome gravity on Earth, you aim high when throwing a ball. In a weightless area you must aim exactly at the spot you want to hit since there is no gravity to bring the ball down. If you drop a ball—or anything else—it won't fall as it will on Earth but will float away in any direction, up, down, or sideways. Running wouldn't be the same either. Once you are in motion at zero-gravity it is almost impossible to change direction, speed up, or slow down without some help. But if you fell, you probably wouldn't hurt yourself. Where there is no gravity no one weighs much and bones seldom break. There could be no swimming pool in the weightless area since water would not stay in the pool. It would float upwards and, like all liquids in space, would

form a perfect sphere or ball. Any food, liquid or solid, taken in the weightless areas would have to be sucked out of tubes or it too would float away.

Life on the station in the areas where there is earth-gravity would be very much like life on Earth. Of course, the colonists could choose the place on Earth they would most like their colony to be like — mountains, lakes, winter or summer all the time. There would be no storms except carefully controlled ones for entertainment, and no activity would have to be called off because of the weather. The stars could be seen, through special viewers, all the time, even during the day. And because they would not be dimmed by Earth's atmosphere, the stars would be much brighter and would show their true colors rather than looking all white. The Moon would seem to be much larger and brighter, but Earth-viewing would be the favorite entertainment. Astronauts say that lightning storms on Earth, seen from above, are exciting beyond belief. Most of the time the colonists would not feel that they were "in space." But when they look through a viewer to see the Earth and the Moon hanging in a black sky in the midst of red, green, and blue stars, they will know they are on another world. A new world in space.

Glossary

Astronomy   The science of the universe and of all the *celestial bodies* within it. It is the oldest of all the sciences.

Atmosphere   All of the gases surrounding a planet; the air of a planet. The atmosphere of Earth goes a hundred miles out from the planet's surface. Two moons, one of Jupiter and one of Saturn, have been found to have an atmosphere.

Celestial body   Celestial means anything related to the heavens or the sky. Celestial bodies are all of the natural objects in space, but the term is most often used about the larger bodies—the suns, the planets, and the moons.

Crater   A large bowl-shaped hole or depression in the surface of a planet or moon. The Moon is heavily cratered. Some of the craters were caused by the explosion of lunar volcanos, but most are the result of meteors crashing into the Moon. The Moon, and possibly Mercury, Venus, Earth, and Mars were heavily bombarded with meteors about four billion years ago.

Dense/Density   An object is dense when all the matter, or molecules, from which it is made are crowded tightly together. A ball of iron, for example, has a greater density than a ball, the same size, of sand. Earth, which is a rather solid planet made mostly of iron, nickel, and rock, has a greater density than any of the giant gas planets. The gas giants have almost the same density that water has.

Diameter   The length of a straight line through the center of an object, especially a round object.

Eclipse   At times, as the Moon *revolves* around the Earth, it passes in front of the Sun and blocks it from view on parts of the Earth. This blocking is called an eclipse of the sun or a solar eclipse. When the Sun is completely covered, the eclipse is called total. More often, however, the Moon only covers part of the sun—a partial eclipse. Mercury and Venus can also pass in front of the Sun, but because the planets are so far away from Earth, they only cover a small section of the Sun. When Mercury or Venus pass between the Earth and the Sun, it is called a transit, not an eclipse.

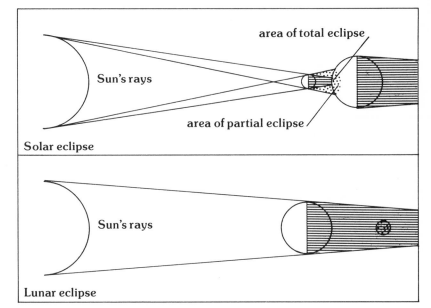

A lunar eclipse takes place when the Moon passes through the Earth's shadow where the Sun's light cannot reach it. The shadow seems to cover the Moon. There are total and partial lunar eclipses.

Galactic/Intergalactic   Both words come from the word galaxy. Galactic means having to do with a galaxy, as in galactic dust or galactic motion. Intergalactic space is the area between galaxies.

Gravity/Gravitational Pull   Gravity is a natural force that pulls all beings and objects "down" toward the center of a *celestial body*. The center of Earth—the center of its gravity—is "down"; everything else is "up." We do not fall off Earth, or any other body with gravity, because to do so we would have to fall up! We are held to the Earth by the force of gravity pulling us down. The gravitational pull, or force, is not the same for all celestial bodies. Jupiter has a very strong gravitational pull, for example, while Mercury has a very weak one. The Sun, of course, has the strongest gravitational pull of any body in our solar system. It is the gravitational force of the Sun that keeps the planets from soaring off into space. Some natural and artificial bodies have no, or very little, gravity. No gravity is called zero-gravity. (See *Weight/Weightlessness*)

Light-year The star nearest to the Sun is 26,000,000,000,000 miles (42,000,000,000,000 kilometers) away. Such large numbers are difficult to say or write without error. A different unit of distance—the light-year—has therefore been used to measure the vast distances of space. The light-year is the distance over which light travels, in a vacuum, in one year—6 million million miles. Stars are usually several light-years apart. The average star is well under one light-minute in *diameter* and our Sun is less than 5 light-seconds in diameter. The term light-year is no longer used by most astronomers since it has not proved precise enough. Within the solar system the unit of measurement is called an Astronomical Unit which is 93,000,000 miles, the approximate distance from the Earth to the Sun. The unit of measurement used beyond the solar system is a parsec which is about 3.26 light-years. For larger distances the kiloparsec and the megaparsec are used.

Mass The amount of material or matter in an object. The Sun has more mass than any body in the solar system. It has 1,047 times the mass of Jupiter, the most massive of the planets. Although the largest bodies are often very massive, mass is not the same as size. The amount of *gravitational pull* of a *celestial body* is related to its mass and its size.

Orbit The path of one body in space around another body, called its primary. Planets are in orbit around the Sun; moons and artificial *satellites* are in orbit around planets. Most orbits are oval—elliptical—in shape since the curve of the orbit must be almost the same as the curve of the planet. If the curve of an orbit were very different from the curve of its primary, the body in orbit might be able to escape the *gravitational pull* and go into space or be forced into the primary's surface by gravitational pull. While in orbit, the body is really "falling" around its primary.

Revolve To move in space in an *orbit* around a *celestial body.* Planets revolve around the Sun. A revolution is the completion of one trip around a body in space by another body.

Rotate To turn or spin on an axis. An axis is an imaginary line, going straight through a *celestial body,* around which the body spins. Both sides of the body, on either side of the axis, must be almost the same weight and shape or the body will wobble as it rotates. The period of rotation is the time it takes a body to make one complete turn on its axis. A planet rotates on its axis as it *revolves* around the Sun.

Satellite A body which *orbits* around another body of larger size and *gravitational pull.* Satellites may be natural, as moons are, or artificial. Spacecraft have become Moon satellites and many artificial satellites are now in orbit around Earth. There is an imaginary line in outer space about 22,300 miles (36,000 kilometers) above the equator of Earth and completely circling the planet. An orbit on this line is the perfect place for artificial communications satellites. Although the line is 165,000 miles (265,000 kilometers) long, it is already crowded. Soon there may be satellite traffic jams in space.

Terrestrial/Extraterrestrial Terrestrial refers to anything related to Earth and its inhabitants. Five of the planets—Mercury, Venus, Earth, Mars, and Pluto—are called terrestrial because they are earth-like in comparison to the giant gas planets. Anything that does not originally come from Earth is called extraterrestrial. Meteorites, asteroids, and space debris that collide with Earth are all extraterrestrial, even though they are now on Earth. If there is life on another planet, that life form would be called extraterrestrial.

Weight/Weightlessness Weight is caused by gravity. A rock that weighs 60 pounds on Earth weighs that because the Earth is pulling at it with 60 pounds of gravitational force. The same rock will weigh only 10 pounds on the Moon since the Moon's gravity is only one-sixth that of the Earth's. The moon can pull at the rock with only 10 pounds of gravitational force. When a person or an object is somewhere, as on a spacecraft, that has no gravity, that person or object will have no weight. One of the problems of weightlessness is that people and things float away. Astronauts in the Skylabs had to tie down objects and fasten themselves to floors and walls with hooks.

115322

DATE DUE

MAR 0 9 '82		
FEB 0 9 1983		
MAY		
APR 2 3 1990		
MAY 1 0 1990		
DEC 2 6 1997		
MAY 0 5 1999		
DEC 0 5 2001		
MAY 1 8		

J
520
S
Sarnoff, Jane
Space: a fact and riddle book.

Ohio Dominican College Library
1216 Sunbury Road
Columbus, Ohio 43219

DEMCO